SELF-AID

Inspirations to Turn Struggles into Success

"Put your heart, mind and soul into even your smallest acts. This is the secret to success."
Swami Sivananda

"Each and every one of us is put on earth here to make a difference. It is our duty to let our individuality shine."
Wooism

Helen Woo

*Self-Aid – Inspirations to Turn
Struggles into Success*

Helen Woo

Published by:
RockStar Publishing House
32129 Lindero Canyon Road, Suite 205
Westlake Village, CA 91361

www.rockstarpublishinghouse.com

Copyright © 2015 Helen Woo

All rights reserved. No part of this book may be reproduced or transmitted in any form or by in any means, electronic or mechanical, including photocopying, recording, or by any information storage and retrieval system, without the written permission of the Publisher, except where permitted by law.

Manufactured in the United States of America, or in the United Kingdom when distributed elsewhere.

Author: Woo, Helen
  Self-Aid – Inspirations to Turn Struggles into Success
  ISBN: 978-1-93750-6889 paperback
  ISBN: 978-1-93750-6896 eBook
  ISBN: 978-1-93750-6902 hardcover
  Library of Congress: 2014958830

Cover design by: John Ballman

Cover photo by: Robert Raphael

Interior design: Dawn Teagarden

Editing by: Teresa Velardi

This book is not intended as a substitute for the medical advice of physicians. The reader should regularly consult a physician in matters relating to his/her mental, physical or emotional health and particularly with respect to any symptoms that may require diagnosis or medical attention.

www.SelfAidwithHelenWoo.com   www.HelenWooToday.com

I dedicate this book to my angel, Ayden, my gift from God. You teach me daily, the power of unconditional love. I thank you for making me laugh often and for keeping me young. You are a true incentive for my progression every day. This book came to fruition because of you, My Sweet Boy.

4

CONTENTS

Foreword...7

Acknowledgment...11

Introduction...13

Chapter 1 — SELF-AID:
I can help myself to live a better life. 15

Chapter 2 — ESTEEM:
Confidence is a gift. 31

Chapter 3 (Part One) — LOVE:
Is everything to me. 51

Chapter 3 (Part Two) — LAUGHTER:
Laugh a little, laugh a lot. Just don't forget to laugh. 75

Chapter 4 — FREEDOM:
Get rid of your baggage, and let go of
negative emotions. Say good bye to the past. 91

Chapter 5 — ATTITUDE:
Mindset is reflected in your attitude. Make yours
one of positive thinking and gratitude. 107

Chapter 6 — INTEGRITY:
I am what I say I am,
and I let my actions define me. 121

Chapter 7 — DREAM:
My life is the result of my dreams. 133

Chapter 8 — GRATITUDE:
Every day is Thanksgiving. Today's affirmation:
I will have an attitude of gratitude. 149

Postscript 163

About the Author 165

Book Review 167

FOREWORD

Having been in the personal development industry for almost 30 years as a speaker and trainer around the world, once in a great while, we come across a body of work that encompasses both an assemblance of outcome-based strategies as well as an empathetic depth of understanding. Helen Woo has crafted just such a book.

Moving through life requires knowledge of each and every moment that connects to create hours, days, weeks, years, decades, and lifetimes. You are a unique individual. You are a compilation of many different facets.

In *"Self Aid – Inspirations to Turn Struggles into Success,"* Helen Woo breaks down, with a simplistic style, just how to identify and explore common components of life and to build each area allowing you to create the best version of you. Helen's unique approach combines the elements of self-esteem, self-image, personal triumph and their unique correlation to a life by design.

In life, we often look outside ourselves for the answers. Each chapter in this book will peel the layers away and allow an introspective look into building blocks required to create greatness within ourselves. It makes no difference whether you are an introvert, extrovert, young, old, male or female. Reading this book will bring forth your capacity to change. You will learn to laugh at yourself, applaud yourself, question yourself and begin to see with clarity exactly how to craft your own path on life's journey.

This book will allow you to become your own best friend, your own best cheerleader, and encourage you to love yourself in a way that resonates with others and will positively affect everyone you come in contact with.

Read this book and read it again. Acquire the information, assimilate it and apply it. Get a copy to everyone you know. Taking action gives you the power to change the world. You now have in your hands a

Chapter 1—FOREWORD

blueprint on how to get out of your own way, become your most powerful ally, and positively affect those around you. This book is a priceless contribution to everyone.

To Your Masterpiece.

Jim Lutes

Author of *The Change* and *Life Masterpiece*

www.lutesinternational.com

ACKNOWLEDGMENT

This book was created from the love and support of many special people in my life.

First and foremost, I want to thank my sweet Little Helen Cheng and my Superman Boone Chou. You have continued to give me relentless support through the years. When I fell hard and felt completely broken, you were always there to hold my hand and help me pick up the pieces. Thank you for always having faith in me and for validating that friendship consists of true, unconditional love.

Thank you to the public figures of today and yesterday, the thinkers and the philosophers who have touched my heart and taught me the power of the word. Your words – many of them in this book – continue to empower me to reach for the stars.

Thank you, Ellen Degeneres, for inspiring me daily and for reminding me of the power behind laughter.

Self-Aid: Inspirations to Turn Struggles into Success

Special thanks to Jim Lutes for writing my foreword. Thank you for your insight and inspiration. I am grateful for your kind words.

Glenn Morshower, my mentor, I thank you for making me laugh and having faith in me that I can always go the extra mile. I will always appreciate you for your sunny disposition. Thank you for writing my review.

Special thanks to Teresa Velardi, my editor, Karen Strauss, my publisher, and my peers in the Rockstar Mastermind group. Thank you, Karen Bailey and Kim Somers Egelsee for writing my book reviews.

Thank you, to my wonderful child, Ayden. Thank you, Ma Ma, Ba Ba (Mom and Dad). Thank you, Katie McGinnis, Susan Kastner, Carina Delgado, Darlyn Chou, Donna Paterson, Taajalea, Pauline and Allen Kay, and David C. for your support especially through the trying times.

To those I've mentioned above, and to all my Dear Friends and Family, far and near, who are too many to list, I appreciate you more than you know, for your love and support. I send right back to you all my love and gratitude tenfold!

I am forever grateful to you.

Helen

INTRODUCTION

I create my *Wooisms* from the inspiration that I seek and receive every day.

Wooisms are positive thoughts and words that empower me to overcome my struggles and inspire me to look for the light when I feel trapped in the darkness.

Wooisms are also my personal affirmations. They help me achieve more daily and motivate me to take action when needed.

Although *Wooisms* are my thoughts put into my own words, they are created by the inspiration that I gratefully receive from many great minds along the way.

My wish for you is that you come to a realization that everything you've been through or are going through today was put in your life to give you strength and allow you to find your personal resolve.

This book, *Self-Aid —Inspirations to Turn Struggles into Success*, is filled with an abundance of inspiring thoughts and words that I hope will encourage you to live the life that you were meant to live: a beautiful one.

A little bit of *Self-Aid* a day can keep the ugly away. May you experience pure exuberation in your life and find the beauty that is in YOU.

It is my hope that this book touches your heart, makes you smile, gives you confidence and encourages you to live the life of your dreams today and EVERY day.

I believe in *Self-Aid*, and I believe in you.

Helen Woo

CHAPTER ONE

SELF-AID:
I can help myself to live a better life.

I didn't always know this. I was absorbed in what everyone else thought my life should be; until I realized that I needed to work on myself, and make me a better me. Now, what you see is what you get; and that's the "real" me. Self-improvement is a priority.

> **self-aid:**
> *n. the act of helping yourself, the act of assisting yourself, the act of giving to yourself, the means of self-remedying.*
>
> *v. to help oneself, to aid, to make better*

"Self-care is never a selfish act—it is simply good stewardship of the only gift I have, the gift I was put on earth to offer to others."

Parker Palmer

"When I came to a realization that 'Self-Aid' is not selfishness but a necessity, I gained the desire to improve myself daily. I realized that there were so many areas of my life that I needed to work on every day. Now I feel stronger and more confident about my actions and above all, I feel I have been given the greatest gift of all: the gift of being able to help others."

Wooism

"Don't wait around for other people to be happy for you. Any happiness you get you've got to make yourself."

Alice Walker

"I am in control of my own happiness. Nothing and no one can stop me from living a happy life."

Wooism

"Everything around us is made up of energy. To attract positive things in your life, start by giving off positive energy."

Author unknown

"Positive thoughts produce my positive actions. I trained my mind and made it a habit to think good thoughts, and now I continually see good results."

Wooism

"Happiness depends upon ourselves."
Aristotle

"I used to make excuses for all my faults and mistakes that I made, and I blamed everyone but myself. I was unable to achieve more or to improve myself. Then I realized that if I stopped playing the victim, things would turn around for me. I am the victor now, and I am able to manifest my own happiness."
Wooism

"The human experience spares no one yet offers all a perspective."
Jim Lutes

"We are all affected by life's challenges. However, if we explore the possibilities of triumph, we will find our way out of the maze, sooner than later."
Wooism

Self-Aid: Inspirations to Turn Struggles into Success

"Life is an opportunity, benefit from it.

Life is beauty, admire it.
Life is bliss, taste it.
Life is a dream, realize it.
Life is a challenge, meet it.
Life is a duty, complete it.
Life is a game, play it.
Life is a promise, fulfill it.
Life is sorrow, overcome it.
Life is a song, sing it.
Life is a struggle, accept it.
Life is a tragedy, confront it.
Life is an adventure, dare it.
Life is luck, make it.
Life is too precious, do not destroy it.
Life is life, fight for it."

Mother Teresa

"Today's affirmation: My life is precious. I have the ability to create greatness throughout my lifetime. I am here today to be the best that I can be. I want to take every opportunity to help myself reach my full potential. This is my life, and I cherish it."

Wooism

Chapter 1—SELF-AID: I can help myself to live a better life.

"Positive self-direction is the action that all winners in life use to turn imagination into reality, fantasy into fact, and dreams into actual goals."
Denis Waitley

"In order to live my dream, I believe in taking one step at a time. If I make an effort, I will reach my goals. I am here, I am ready, and I am willing."
Wooism

"It is one of the most beautiful compensations of this life that no man can sincerely try to help another without helping himself."
Ralph Emerson

"Just as I must put on my oxygen mask before being able to help my child on an airplane, in my everyday life, I must take care of me first, so that I can be of assistance to others. What good am I if I do not take care of myself?"
Wooism

"*Difficulties mastered are opportunities won.*"
Winston Churchill

"Each challenge I overcome gets me
one step closer to a better me."
Wooism

"*Put your heart, mind and soul into even your smallest acts.
This is the secret of success.*"
Swami Sivananda

"When I put passion into even the smallest acts,
I am rewarded with happiness."
Wooism

"*You can't always change your situation,
but you can change your attitude.*"
Larry Hargraves

"Instead of complaining that my life is difficult
and that nothing ever goes my way, I'd rather
believe that anything is possible."
Wooism

Chapter 1—SELF-AID: I can help myself to live a better life.

"Let us not be content to wait and see what will happen, but give us the determination to make the right things happen."
Peter Marshall

"I cannot read into the future; however, I can be proactive now and create my own fate."
Wooism

"I am always doing that I which I cannot do, in order that I may learn how to do it."
Pablo Picasso

"I was not given instant knowledge at birth, but I am capable; and therefore, I am more skilled than I was yesterday."
Wooism

"The measure of a man is the way he bears up under misfortune."
Plutarch

"I have suffered and I have struggled, and I have made many mistakes. I can drown myself in sorrow, or I can get up, conquer and win."
Wooism

*"A journey of a thousand miles
begins with a single step."*

Chinese Proverb

*"I can repeat the same mistakes over and over,
or I can get out of my comfort zone today and
make a change toward progression."*

Wooism

*"I do not think much of a man who is not
wiser today than he was yesterday."*

Abraham Lincoln

*"I made mistakes because I am human. I repeated mistakes
because I was afraid of change. I changed because
I finally grew tiresome of being ignorant."*

Wooism

*"Most folks are just as happy as they
make up their minds to be."*

Abraham Lincoln

*"I have a choice today. I can sob and complain,
or I can smile and make it a great day. I believe
I am wise to opt for the ladder."*

Wooism

*"Knowledge of what is possible is
the beginning of happiness."*
George Santayana

*"I believe in hope. I believe in all the possibilities
of tomorrow. I know that great things await me,
and I plan to enjoy my journey."*
Wooism

*"There are no great limits to growth because there are no limits
of human intelligence, imagination, and wonder."*
Ronald Reagan

*"If I played it safe and lived a life of monotony,
I may not have encountered all my struggles and defeats;
but nor would I have discovered my passion and
experienced the greatness that lies within me."*
Wooism

*"Do you want to know who you are? Don't ask. Act.
Action will delineate and define you."*
Thomas Jefferson

*"I am transparent. I believe in being true to me and to others,
in public and in private. I cannot see myself any other way."*
Wooism

"Happiness is not being pained in body or troubled in mind."
Thomas Jefferson

"When I make an effort to take good care of myself and laugh often, I find myself happy in body, mind and soul."
Wooism

"A man is but the product of his thoughts; what he thinks, he becomes."
Gandhi

"I know from past experience: the power of positive thinking. Throughout all the hardships, if I did not learn to train my brain, I may have been suicidal."
Wooism

"Happiness is when what you think, what you say, and what you do are in harmony."
Gandhi

"Today's affirmation: I am here to live a blissful life. I promise to match my words with my thoughts, and follow accordingly with my actions."
Wooism

Chapter 1—SELF-AID: I can help myself to live a better life.

"Love begins at home, and it is not how much we do... but how much love we put in that action."
Mother Teresa

"Get to know me, and you will be able to feel my heart and look deep into my soul, for you will see nothing less than passion."
Wooism

"Be not afraid of growing slowly. Be afraid of standing still."
Chinese Proverb

"I can stay the yester me; however, I prefer the wiser, more beautiful version. Stagnant or dynamic? The choice is simple."
Wooism

"You must be the change you want to see in the world."
Gandhi

"I have found my life purpose, and I believe it is time I put my stamp on this planet."
Wooism

"No one saves us but ourselves. No one can and no one may. We ourselves must walk the path."
Buddha

"Denial is an excuse we use when we do not want to admit we did something wrong. It keeps us from taking 100% responsibility for our lives. Today, I admit my faults, I admit defeat, and I admit when I am wrong. This is my life, and I take ownership of it."
Wooism

"The mind is everything. What you think, you become."
Buddha

"Due to life's challenges and much negative thinking, I fell into a depression years ago. A gal name Ellen Degeneres brought laughter back into my life. I was encouraged to surround myself with more inspiration. Today, I fill my mind with positive thoughts. I want to be happy, and so I am."
Wooism

Chapter 1—SELF-AID: I can help myself to live a better life.

> *"Action may not always bring happiness;
> but there is no happiness without action."*
> ### **Benjamin Disraeli**

> *"My destination is 'Happy', and from this day forward,
> I will do what it takes to get there."*
> ### **Wooism**

> *"The purpose of our lives is to be happy."*
> ### **Dalai Lama**

> *"A sense of humor is a powerful tool.
> Make me laugh, and you've made my day."*
> ### **Wooism**

> *"A man cannot be comfortable without his own approval."*
> ### **Mark Twain**

> *"If believe I can, I can."*
> ### **Wooism**

"Apparently, there is nothing that cannot happen today."
Mark Twain

"I have passion, and I have resilience. I can make it happen. Anything is possible."
Wooism

"Take the first step in faith. You don't have to see the whole staircase, just take the first step."
Martin Luther King, Jr.

"I do not have all the details yet, as I cannot see the future. But I have no doubt that greatness lies ahead. How do I know this? Because my 'knowing' lies in the core of my 'being'."
Wooism

"The human mind is our fundamental resource."
John F. Kennedy

"If my mind can think it, my body can do it."
Wooism

Chapter 1—SELF-AID: I can help myself to live a better life.

"There are risks and costs to action. But they are far less than the long range risks of comfortable inaction."
John F. Kennedy

"If I want results, I will make it happen. I know there will be challenges along the way. However, if I start now, I will reach my goals sooner than later."
Wooism

"Things do not happen. Things are MADE to happen."
John F. Kennedy

"Self-Aid is about me helping myself to reach my full potential. I will help myself to achieve ultimate success."
Wooism

"The only source of knowledge is experience."
Albert Einstein

"The best education comes from living through difficult times. Making mistakes and learning to fight my challenges have taught me life's many lessons. From my lessons, I have gained courage and great knowledge."
Wooism

"There are no great limits to growth
because there are no limits of human intelligence,
imagination and wonder."
Ronald Reagan

"The world is my oyster. There is so much to gain and so much to explore throughout this lifetime. Why stop learning when there are infinite possibilities?"
Wooism

"The moment in between what you once were, and who you are now becoming, is where the dance of life really takes place."
Barbara de Angelis

"I cherish each moment and each task in front of me. Although it's not always easy, I appreciate the steps because these moments are part of the transition to building my character."
Wooism

CHAPTER TWO

ESTEEM:
Confidence is a gift.

I wasn't always as confident as I am today. I have twisted and turned as I traveled the road of life. Today, although there are bumps along the way, I have found confidence in who I am and my ability to make good choices and decisions for myself and my family.

esteem:

n. favorable opinion or judgment; respect or regard: to hold a person in esteem.

self-esteem:

n. feeling of personal capacity combined with a feeling of personal worth, self-confidence,

"To me, beauty is about being comfortable in your own skin. It's about knowing who you are and accepting who are you."
Ellen Degeneres

"I think that when we like ourselves, it shows. Confidence allows us to radiate beauty from the inside out."
Wooism

"Confidence is beautiful. No matter your size, no matter your weight… Be confident with who you are and you'll be beautiful."
Unknown

"Beauty comes from within…
If you believe you have it, you have it."
Wooism

"Your persistence is your measure of faith in yourself."
Unknown

"Giving up is not an option. I believe in me, and I know that I will experience victory."
Wooism

"No matter what age you are, or what your circumstances might be, you are special, and you still have something unique to offer. Your life, because of who you are, has meaning."
Barbara de Angelis

"No one is in control of my happiness but I myself; therefore, I have the power to change and improve anything about me that I see necessary. I am one of a kind, and I will continue to polish the special gift that I am."
Wooism

"Persons of high self-esteem are not driven to make themselves superior to others; they do not seek to prove their value by measuring themselves against a comparative standard. Their joy is being who they are, not in being better than someone else."
Nathaniel Branden

"I am unique and very different from the rest. Why choose to be a carbon copy of someone else when I can appreciate and offer the world the one and only me?"
Wooism

"My haters are my motivators."
Ellen DeGeneres

"Lack of faith from others will only give me ammunition to work harder and strive for more. I will create success through my own merit; I appreciate any support, but one's approval is not necessary if I know I'm doing my best."
Wooism

"With realization of one's own potential and self-confidence in one's own ability, one can build a better world."
Dalai Lama

"It is in my blood. I know that I can make a difference. I was born with originality. I was born with a purpose. I will create greatness simply because I believe in myself."
Wooism

"Make sure the outside of you is a good reflection of the inside of you."
Jim Rohn

"Because I love myself, I will nurture my body as well as my soul."
Wooism

"Take the first step in faith. You don't have to see the whole staircase, just take the first step."
Martin Luther King, Jr.

"I believe in myself, and I hope and dream for a brighter tomorrow. One action at a time, I know that I am creating greatness. My progression starts today, and success is my result."
Wooism

"We are all miracle workers; we have within us a Divine capacity. In order to accomplish something, you must first expect it of yourself. And that is one of the reasons that so many people are stuck at ordinary – because they don't have expectations of themselves to go beyond that, to live at an extraordinary level."
Dr. Wayne Dyer

"My ability to accomplish my goals comes from having faith in myself and my Higher Power. I am here not by accident but for a purpose. And I am unstoppable."
Wooism

"Belief actually creates the actual fact."
William James

"I believe I can, and I so I shall."
Wooism

"Look within. Within is the fountain of good, and it will ever bubble up, if thou wilt ever dig."

Marcus Aurelius

"If I search deep within myself, I will find the key that enables the good in me to turn into greatness."

Wooism

"Learn how to carry a friendship greatly, whether or not it is returned. Why should one regret if the receiver is not equally generous? It never troubles the sun that some of his rays fall wide and vain into ungrateful space, and only a small part on the reflecting planet. Let your greatness educate the crude and cold companion. If he is unequal, he will presently pass away; but thou art enlarged by thy own shining."

Ralph Waldo Emerson

"I make a great effort to give generously to myself and to others. My actions come straight from my heart, and I expect nothing in return. Goodness follows me because I am good."

Wooism

Chapter 2—ESTEEM: Confidence is a gift.

"*Do not overrate what you have received, nor envy others. He who envies others does not obtain peace of mind.*"
Buddha

"I remain humble as I nurse my talents and gifts. I have the highest respect and appreciation for the greatness I see in others, and through them, I will learn and grow."
Wooism

"Be who you are and say what you feel, because those who mind don't matter and those who matter don't mind."
Theodore Seuss Giesel (aka Dr.Seuss)

"I shall not waste time worrying about what others think of me. How I feel about myself and what I can do to better myself shall remain my main concerns."
Wooism

"We are each gifted in a unique and important way. It is our privilege and our adventure to discover our own special light."
Mary Dunbar

"I am worth it, and I shall embrace my talents and my gifts and my individuality."
Wooism

*"When people believe in themselves they
have the first secret of success."*

Norman Vincent Peale

*"Confidence: I can accomplish any task put forth upon me
because I believe in me."*

Wooism

*"Don't you dare, for one more second, surround yourself with
people who are not aware of the greatness that you are."*

Jo Blackwell-Preston

*"I have chosen to free myself from the negative banter of
those who look down upon me. Today, I have a great support
system, and I find myself in good company."*

Wooism

*"Your chances of success in any undertaking can always be
measured by your belief in yourself."*

Robert Collier

*"I can overcome all challenges in my life because I will never
give up. I believe in me, and I believe in persistence."*

Wooism

Chapter 2—ESTEEM: Confidence is a gift.

"*I wish I could show you, when you are lonely or in darkness, the astonishing light of your own being."*
Hafiz

"When I reached my lowest low, I discovered the hidden strength within myself. Today, I continue to use this power to help me fight my daily battles."
Wooism

"*To be beautiful means to be yourself. You don't need to be accepted by others. You need to accept yourself."*
Thich Nhat Hanh

"Daily reminder: I do not need to change my ways to impress others; I need to think and act from my heart to impress me. I shall live my life not according to what others ask or think of me; I shall live according to what I think of myself. I have a big heart, and I have integrity. To me, these qualities make me 'enough'."
Wooism

"You are very powerful, provided you know
how powerful you are."

Yogi Bhajan

"I have weathered the toughest storms... I was left with
strength and courage, persistence and endurance, and I have
decided to leave all weakness behind."

Wooism

"Tell me how a person judges his or her self-esteem and I will
tell you how that person operates at work, in love, in sex, in
parenting, in every important aspect of existence – and how
high he or she is likely to rise. The reputation you have
with yourself – your self-esteem – is the single
most important factor for a fulfilling life."

Nathaniel Branden

"I hold myself in the highest regard. Make no mistake,
for I exude not arrogance but a hearty dose of confidence."

Wooism

Chapter 2—ESTEEM: Confidence is a gift.

*"Having a low opinion of yourself is not "modesty".
It's self-destruction. Holding your uniqueness in high regard
is not "egotism". It's a necessary precondition to
happiness and success."*

Bobbe Sommer

*"Self-esteem is in my blood.
Without it, I experience a lack of life."*

Woosim

*"Most of the shadows of this life are caused by
standing in one's own sunshine."*

Ralph Waldo Emerson

*"I have discovered the light within myself.
I am a gem and I shine proudly."*

Woosim

*"You yourself, as much as anybody in the entire universe,
deserve your love and affection."*

Buddha

"I am worthy of my love."

Wooism

"Of all the judgments we pass in life, none is more important than the judgment we pass on ourselves."
Nathaniel Branden

"I find that I am not productive when I put myself down. Rather, when I praise myself, I allow myself to be happy; and ultimately, I am able to conquer the task at hand."
Wooism

"People are like stained-glass windows. They sparkle and shine when the sun is out, but when the darkness sets in, their true beauty is revealed only if there is light from within."
Elisabeth Kübler-Ross

"I spent years trying to find my true self. Today, I am transparent when I express love to myself and to others; and in return, I am able to receive an abundance of love."
Wooism

"Everybody is unique. Compare not yourself with anybody else lest you spoil God's curriculum."
Rabbi Israel ben Eliezer

"I have only one true competitor. That is I, myself."
Wooism

Chapter 2—ESTEEM: Confidence is a gift.

"All things splendid have been achieved by those who dared believe that something inside them was superior to circumstance."
Bruce Barton

"I know that I am unique, and I have a purpose here. I plan to use my God-given talents along with my new knowledge to give back to this world."
Wooism

"By being yourself, you put something wonderful in the world that was not there before."
Edwin Elliot

"I may be different; but I embrace my corkiness and my individuality; and I know there is plenty of room for me to make my mark in this world."
Wooism

"If you hear a voice within you say "You cannot paint," then by all means paint, and that voice will be silenced."
Vincent Van Gogh

*"I am stronger than my fears.
All I have to do is take a chance."*
Wooism

43

'The snow goose need not bathe to make itself white. Neither need you do anything but be yourself."
Lao-Tzu

"I do not need to be like anyone else. There is no room for envy, as I appreciate who I am and who I am becoming. Being myself is enough."
Wooism

"The way you treat yourself sets the standard for others."
Sonya Friedman

"Self-respect enables me to earn respect from others."
Wooism

"Self-care is never a selfish act – it is simply good s tewardship of the only gift I have, the gift I was put on earth to offer to others."
Parker Palmer

"Self-love and self-nourishment are my priorities... There is no better way to help others than to help myself first."
Wooism

Chapter 2—ESTEEM: Confidence is a gift.

"*The privilege of a lifetime is being who you are.*"
Joseph Campbell

"*There is only one of me, and I am grateful
and honored to be just that.*"
Wooism

"*The strongest single factor in acquiring abundance is self-esteem: believing you can do it, believing you deserve it, believing you will get it.*"
Jerry Gillies

"*I believe in me and my abilities; therefore, I can accomplish anything I set myself to do.*"
Wooism

"*Remember always that you not only have the right to be an individual, you have an obligation to be one.*"
Eleanor Roosevelt

"*I love that I am different. I love that I am one of a kind. And only I can bring out the wonders of my own individuality.*"
Wooism

"Accept yourself as you are. Otherwise you will never see opportunity. You will not feel free to move toward it; you will feel you are not deserving."
Maxwell Maltz

"Today I will give myself love, nurture and approval. I am worthy and deserving. Yes, I am."
Wooism

"Learn to value yourself, which means: to fight for your happiness."
Ayn Rand

"It is my responsibility to create the outcome that I want. I am deserving of happiness, and so I shall have it."
Wooism

"You can't build joy on a feeling of self-loathing."
Ram Dass

"Forgiving myself is important because it opens a new pathway for me love myself; and it enables me to experience true happiness."
Wooism

Chapter 2—ESTEEM: Confidence is a gift.

"It's not your job to like me…it's MINE!"
Byron Katie

"I seek my own approval before anyone else's. It's not you I need to impress; it's me. After all, I am worthy."
Wooism

"To establish true self-esteem, we must concentrate on our successes and forget about the failures and the negatives in our lives."
Denis Waitley

"Bouncing back from my failures and downfalls have molded me into the person that I am today. I am stronger and wiser than ever, and I can conquer anything now."
Wooism

"High self-esteem isn't a luxury. It's a necessity for anyone who has goals to achieve."
Jack Canfield

"Self-esteem is an obligation. To accomplish anything in life, I live, breathe and believe I can."
Wooism

"As you grow in self-esteem, your face, manner, way of talking and moving will tend naturally to project the pleasure you take in being alive."
Nathaniel Branden

"Confidence shows in your walk and in your talk. People around you will hear it in your words and see it in your actions. They feel your exhilaration for life and hope that some of it rubs off on them, too."
Wooism

"Sooner or later, those who win are those who think they can."
Richard Bach

"All great accomplishments come from individuals with high self-esteem."
Wooism

"Self-esteem is as necessary to the spirit as it is to the body."
Dr. Maxwell Maltz

"When you feel confident on the inside, you radiate confidence on the outside."
Wooism

Chapter 2—ESTEEM: Confidence is a gift.

"*The will to do springs from the knowledge that we can do.*"
James Allen

"Like the Little Engine that Could, I think I can, I think I can."
Wooism

"*Whether you think you can or whether you think you cannot – you are right.*"
Henry Ford

"My mind today is set to 'positive' and I know that anything is possible."
Wooism

"*Self-pity is our worst enemy, and if we yield to it, we can never do anything wise in the world.*"
Helen Keller

"My time shall not be wasted on feeling sorry for myself because I am competent, and I am enough."
Wooism

"I was once afraid of people saying, 'Who does she think she is?' Now I have the courage to stand and say, 'This is who I am.'"
Oprah Winfrey

"I used to make it a priority to have others like me and approve of me. I chose to say and do the right things at the right times, all according to what they expected from me. I have since realized that it is my own approval that matters the most to me. Today, I speak and act from my heart, and I start by liking me."
Wooism

"To me, beauty is about being comfortable in your own skin. It's about knowing and accepting who you are."
Ellen Degeneres

"Each and every one of us is beautiful. We just have to believe we are; the more we believe, the more attractive we become."
Wooism

CHAPTER THREE
(PART ONE)

LOVE:
is everything to me.

It is the love of a child, the love of a parent and the love of oneself. It is the tenderness and passion of a relationship with a partner or a friend. It is the time spent with someone in need or sharing the joy of a good laugh. It is the passion underlying everything that is me. True love comes from the unconditional love of God.

love:

n. a strong emotion, a profoundly tender affection, a feeling of warm personal attachment or deep affection, love is a virtue representing all of human kindness, compassion, and affection.

v. to have love and affection for, to feel the emotion of love.

"Love is the most passionate force of nature. Once we experience it, we spend our life wanting to give and receive more."

Wooism

"Love is a force more formidable than any other. It is invisible - it cannot be seen or measured, yet it is powerful enough to transform you in a moment, and offer you more joy than any material possession could."

Barbara de Angelis

"Living life without love is living in emptiness."

Wooism

"For it was not into my ears you whispered, but into my heart. It was not my lips you kissed, but my soul."

Judy Garland

"The way you look at me, the way you speak to me, the way you give to me intoxicates me... I feel your passion and you feel mine. There is no doubt that love exists."

Wooism

Chapter 3 (Part 2)—LOVE: is everything to me.

"People are like stain-glass windows. They sparkle and shine when the sun is out, but when the darkness sets in, their true beauty is revealed only if there is light from within."
Elisabeth Kübler-Ross

"I spent years looking for and finally discovering my true self. Today, I am transparent; I am able to give and receive love in abundance because I come from a place called love."
Wooism

"Try to be a rainbow in someone's cloud."
Maya Angelou

"It takes no effort to make someone feel good. Give a little love today; put on a smile."
Wooism

"Love is the master key that opens the gates of happiness."
Oliver Wendall Holmes

"The absolute most passionate gift of nature is love. Love is life."
Wooism

"Love is a fabric which never fades, no matter how often it is washed in the water of adversity and grief."
Author Unknown

"Love is stronger than any defeat. Love is power."
Wooism

"Love comforteth like sunshine after rain."
William Shakespeare

"Love diminishes my worries and keeps me optimistic. Love enables me to see the possibilities."
Wooism

"Paradise is always where love dwells."
Jean Paul F. Richter

"To experience love is to have a taste of heaven on earth."
Wooism

Chapter 3 (Part 2)—LOVE: is everything to me.

"Appreciation and self-love are the most important tools that you could ever nurture. Appreciation of others, and the appreciation of yourself is the closest vibrational match to your Source Energy of anything that we've ever witnessed anywhere in the Universe."

Abraham

"Love teaches many lessons. Loving yourself and others is only part of the journey. Love is caring, love is giving, love is healing. The more love you give in this world, the more you receive."

Wooism

"Love is patient, love is kind. It does not envy, it does not boast, it is not proud. It is not rude, it is not self-seeking, it is not easily angered, it keeps no record of wrongs. Love does not delight in evil but rejoices with the truth. It always protects, always trusts, always hopes, always perseveres."

Corinthians

"Love is a gift we possess that not only wins every battle for us, it nourishes our souls."

Wooism

*"There is so much love in your heart
that you could heal the planet."*
Louise Hay

"Love opens our hearts and allows us recognize the wondrous miracles that come in every day."
Wooism

"Self-love, is not so vile a sin as self-neglecting."
William Shakespeare

"To find harmony in body, mind and soul, I must love myself enough to take care of me today."
Wooism

"A *life without love in it is like a heap of ashes upon a deserted hearth, with the fire dead, the laughter stilled and the light extinguished."*
Frank Tebbets

"Life without love is life without a purpose."
Wooism

Chapter 3 (Part 2)—LOVE: is everything to me.

*"Love is the great miracle cure.
Loving ourselves works miracles in our lives."*
Louise L.Hay

*"Love teaches, and love heals. Love brings passion
into your life and gives you determination and resilience
when you need them most. Love gives you self-esteem and
faith; for with love, everything is possible. Choose love;
it is the best solution."*
Wooism

*"Keep love in your heart. A life without it is like a sunless garden
when the flowers are dead."*
Oscar Wilde

*"Love enables me to see the beauty in
everything and everyone."*
Wooism

"Friends can help each other. A true friend is someone who lets you have total freedom to be yourself - and especially to feel. Or, not feel. Whatever you happen to be feeling at the moment is fine with them. That's what real love amounts to – letting a person be what he really is."

Jim Morrison

"Love does not judge, love does not condemn. Love is unconditional at its best; love creates true friendships."

Wooism

"I have decided to stick with love. Hate is too great a burden to bear."

Martin Luther King Jr.

"Once you kick anger and resentment out the door, you will see that you are left with love greater than you've ever imagined."

Wooism

Chapter 3 (Part 2)—LOVE: is everything to me.

"Where there is love there is life."
Mahatma Gandhi

"Life is made up of energy; the greatest of them is love."
Wooism

"We loved with a love that was more than love."
Edgar Allan Poe

"The more you love, the bigger your heart gets."
Wooism

"The moment you have in your heart this extraordinary thing called love and feel the depth, the delight, the ecstasy of it, you will discover that for you the world is transformed."
Jiddu Krishnamurti

"There is so much joy that comes with love that I find myself rolling in euphoria."
Wooism

"Love is the beauty of the soul."
Saint Augustine

"Love me for who I am on the inside, as my physical body is only temporary, but my soul is forever."
Wooism

"The way to know life is to love many things."
Vincent Van Gogh

"There is an abundance of love in our hearts to share with the world; we can shine like the stars and light up the Universe."
Wooism

"Happiness is when what you think, what you say, and what you do are in harmony."
Mahatma Gandhi

"Integrity expresses love."
Wooism

Chapter 3 (Part 2)—LOVE: is everything to me.

"One word frees us of all the weight and pain in life: that word is love."

Socrates

"Loves eases pain; love mends a broken heart. Believe in love because it performs miracles."

Wooism

"Love cures people – both the ones who give it and the ones who receive it."

Dr. Karl Menninger

"Love relieves pain and forgives the past. Love prepares you for the greatness that lies ahead."

Wooism

"There is no remedy for love but to love more."
Thoreau

"I am addicted to love."
Wooism

"You yourself, as much as anybody in the entire universe, deserve your love and affection."
Buddha

"Love starts with you, and if you spread a little of it, it continues to spout in all directions."
Wooism

"Love is a mutual self-giving which ends in self-recovery."
Fulton J. Sheen

"Loving myself is not selfishness; it is the greatest gift I can give to myself because by taking care of me, I can be whole and healthy; and therefore, I can be helpful to others."
Wooism

Chapter 3 (Part 2)—LOVE: is everything to me.

"Love is like magic
And it always will be.
For love still remains
Life's sweet mystery!!
Love works in ways
That are wondrous and strange
And there's nothing in life
That love cannot change!!
Love can transform
The most commonplace
Into beauty and splendor
And sweetness and grace.
Love is unselfish,
Understanding and kind,
For it sees with its heart
And not with its mind!!
Love is the answer
That everyone seeks...
Love is the language,
That every heart speaks.
Love can't be bought,
It is priceless and free,
Love, like pure magic,
Is life's sweet mystery!!"

Helen Steiner Rice

"My life is full of love, and I am grateful!"

Wooism

"Love is the master key that opens the gates of happiness."
Oliver Wendall Holmes

"The secret to living a happy life is learning how to give and receive love."
Wooism

"Love is like the sun coming out of the clouds and warming your soul."
Author Unknown

"*Today's affirmation: Smile, because smiling is contagious. I deserve some love today.*"
Wooism

"Love is more than a feeling; it's a state of mind."
Lisa Grude

"*Live passionately and impulsively. Feel the love today and express yourself with your words and actions.*"
Wooism

Chapter 3 (Part 2)—LOVE: is everything to me.

"*Love is like a piece of art work,
even the smallest bit can be so beautiful.*"
Stacie Cunningham

"Love in any measure is magnetic."
Wooism

"*Love is the emblem of eternity; it confounds all notions of time;
effaces all memory of beginning, all fear of an end.*"
Madame de Stael

"Love in its greatest form is indestructible and everlasting."
Wooism

"*Love is, above all, the gift of oneself.*"
Jean Anouilh

"All great triumphs start with self-love."
Wooism

"Hatred ever kills, love never dies such is the vast difference between the two. What is obtained by love is retained for all time. What is obtained by hatred proves a burden in reality for it increases hatred."

Gandhi

"Love frees anger and resentment; it heals wounds and teaches forgiveness. Love is greater than its enemy because love is good."

Wooism

"It is better to be hated for who you are than to be loved for what you are not."

Andre Gide

"It is not our duty to impress others. However, if our actions are based on love and integrity, we will be surrounded by true friends."

Wooism

"There is no remedy for love but to love more."

Henry David Thoreau

"Love is a natural cure that keeps on giving."

Wooism

Chapter 3 (Part 2)—LOVE: is everything to me.

"Life without love is like a tree without blossoms or fruit."
Kahlil Gibran

"Living without love is living an empty life."
Wooism

"Love is the triumph of imagination over intelligence."
HL Mencken

"When you need to choose between the mind and the heart, continue to follow your passion, as that voice never leads you astray."
Wooism

"One word frees us of all the weight and pain of life: That word is love."
Sophocles

"To the fears, the worries, and the challenges: I will not fall victim to you. I have love by my side."
Wooism

*"To give and not expect in return,
that is what lies at the heart of love."*
Oscar Wilde

"There are no conditions. Love is giving and
love is given with no explanation."
Wooism

"You, yourself, as much as anybody in the entire universe,
deserve your love and affection."
Buddha

"Today's affirmation: I am worthy of all my love."
Wooism

*"Love feels no burden, thinks nothing of trouble, attempts what
is above its strength, pleads no excuse of impossibility; for it
thinks all things lawful for itself, and all things possible."*
Thomas à Kempis

"With love, I am invincible."
Wooism

Chapter 3 (Part 2)—LOVE: is everything to me.

"*Love is the only force capable of transforming an enemy into friend."*
Martin Luther King

"*Love can conquer any battle."*
Wooism

"*It is not how much you do, but how much Love you put into the doing that matters."*
Mother Teresa

"Today's affirmation: Be passionate in all that I do today; by the end of the day, I will be rewarded with more joy than I'd imagined possible."
Wooism

"*The thought manifests as the word. The word manifests as the deed. The deed develops into habit. And the habit hardens into character. So watch the thought and its ways with care. And let it spring from love, born out of concern for all beings."*
Buddha

"Since my actions stem from my thoughts, I will practice positive thinking more often. I plan to manifest many a positive outcome."
Wooism

"Love many things, for therein lies the true strength, and whosoever loves much performs much, and can accomplish much, and what is done in love is done well."
Vincent Van Gogh

"Passion is love working its magic."
Wooism

"A love affair with knowledge will never end in heartbreak."
Michael Garrett Marino

"My aspiration is to become a better version of me. Each day, week, month and year, I love to see the progression I have made for myself."
Wooism

"A heart that loves is always young."
Greek Proverb

"My passion for life gives away my age. Yes, I am quite youthful!"
Wooism

Chapter 3 (Part 2)—LOVE: is everything to me.

"In dreams and in love there are no impossibilities."
Janos Arnay

"Love ignites my passion, and my goals become attainable. Love gives me hope and faith and opens my eyes to all the possibilities."
Wooism

"The best and most beautiful things in this world cannot be seen or even heard, but must be felt with the heart."
Helen Keller

"Where there is love, there is beauty."
Wooism

"Love and kindness are never wasted. They always make a difference."
Babara de Angelis

"Every good deed pays it forward.
Like a smile or a laugh, love is contagious."
Wooism

"Gentleness, self-sacrifice and generosity are the exclusive possessions of no one race or religion."
Gandhi

"Love teaches me kindness and generosity. Love gives me a good name."
Wooism

"When I do good, I feel good. When I do bad, I feel bad. That's my religion."
Abraham Lincoln

"My conscience is filled with one hundred percent love."
Wooism

"I can do everything through Him who gives me strength."
Phil 4:13

"I have an abundance of faith in God, for His love gives me the power of goodness to think, speak and act with conviction."
Wooism

Chapter 3 (Part 2)—LOVE: is everything to me.

*"He who pursues righteousness and
love finds life, prosperity and honor."*
Proverbs 21:21

"One who lives with integrity finds true love."
Wooism

"We can't help everyone, but everyone can help someone."
Ronald Reagan

*"It takes one kind gesture or one kind act to make the
greatest difference in someone's life."*
Wooism

*"I believe that every human mind
feels pleasure in doing good to another."*
Thomas Jefferson

*"Imagine if we all contributed and performed one good deed
a day… the world becomes a happier place instantly."*
Wooism

"*Be kind to one another.*"

Ellen Degeneres

"The Golden Rule is my truth. I make an effort to do unto others as I'd like them to do unto me. This truth is my religion."

Wooism

"*Everyone who wills can hear the inner voice. It is within everyone.*"

Gandhi

"Where we are, God is; where God is, all are loved."

Wooism

"*I believe in the fundamental truth of all great religions of the world.*"

Gandhi

"There is one unified religion; it is called 'Love'."

Wooism

CHAPTER 3
(PART TWO)

LAUGHTER:
Laugh a little, laugh a lot.
Just don't forget to laugh.

Laughter lightens my spirit and is the joy that lives in my soul. It, like love, is a gift of the heart. It is what motivates me to live my life fully and completely.

LAUGHTER

n. the action or sound of laughing, an experience of the emotion expressed by laughing, an expression or appearance of merriment.

"Laughter is the best medicine."
English Proverb

"Laughter relaxes the muscles, boosts energy,
and improves respiration in the body.

Laughter stimulates circulation and reduces stress.

Laughter enables better sleep at night.

Laughter calms negative emotions
such as fear and anger.

Laughter has no unexpected side effects.

Laughter has no maximum dosage,
so there's no chance of overdose.

Laughter comes with no prescription necessary.

Here's another incentive to laugh: Laughter is free.

Laughter is my medicine;
I am grateful for this addiction."
Wooism

"I believe there is a direct correlation
between love and laughter."
Yakov Smirnoff

"One cannot live without the other.
Love with laughter, and laugh with love."
Wooism

Chapter 3 (Part 2)—LAUGHTER: Laugh a little, laugh a lot. Just don't forget to laugh.

"If I were given the opportunity to present a gift to the next generation, it would be the ability for each individual to laugh at himself."

Charles M. Schultz

"Laughing at myself is healthy.
Plus, it takes away any embarrassment."

Wooism

"Always laugh when you can. It is cheap medicine."

Lord Byron

"If I want to be happy, and I'm short on cash, I choose laughter because laughter is instant and laughter is free."

Wooism

"Against the assault of laughter, nothing can stand."

Mark Twain

"Go ahead, try to make me angry.
I'll beat you silly with a dose of laughter."

Wooism

"At the height of laughter, the universe is flung into a kaleidoscope of new possibilities."
Jean Houston

"Laughter is my strength. It gives me optimism when my days are dim. It gives me opportunities when my chances look slim."
Wooism

"There is little success where there is little laughter."
Andrew Carnagie

"Laughter triumphs over defeat."
Wooism

"If love is the treasure, laughter is the key."
Yakov Smirnoff

"Laughter opens up my heart and brings out the passion in me."
Wooism

Chapter 3 (Part 2)—LAUGHTER: Laugh a little, laugh a lot. Just don't forget to laugh.

"Laughter need not be cut out of anything,
since it improves everything."
James Thurber

"I find the most attractive trait about someone is their ability to laugh and to make me laugh, too. That, to me, is a great start to a new friendship."
Wooism

"Laughter relieves us of superfluous energy, which, if it remained unused, might become negative, that is, poison. Laughter is the antidote."
George Gurdjieff

"The best way to get rid of ugly emotions is to start looking into the mirror and start laughing for no reason at all."
Wooism

"Laughter springs from the lawless part of our nature."
Agnes Repplier

"There are no restrictions, no rules and no limit. Laughter is a gift we each possess. To show appreciation, we should laugh more often."
Wooism

"Seven days without laughter makes one weak."
Mort Walker

"Like breathing, laughter is a vital part of existence. Laughter is the spice of life!"
Wooism

"So many tangles in life are ultimately hopeless that we have no appropriate sword other than laughter."
Gordon W. Allport

"In time of grief and sadness, laughing heals."
Wooism

"The sound of laughter is like the vaulted dome of a temple of happiness."
Milan Kundera

"Happiness starts and ends with laughter."
Wooism

Chapter 3 (Part 2)—LAUGHTER: Laugh a little, laugh a lot. Just don't forget to laugh.

"If you can make a girl laugh, you can make her do anything."
Marilyn Monroe

"A sense of humor is a powerful tool.
Make me laugh and I love you."
Wooism

"With mirth and laughter, let old wrinkles come."
William Shakespeare

"I came into this world crying,
but I plan to leave this world laughing."
Wooism

"Let there be more joy and laughter in your living."
Eileen Caddy

"When I hit rock bottom and I felt the world I lived in was
falling apart, I decided to self-medicate. My prescription was
one hour of laughter a day with Ellen Degeneres.
Now that's good medicine."
Wooism

"Live by this credo: Have a little laugh at life and look around for happiness instead of sadness. Laughter has always brought me out of unhappy situations."
Red Skelton

"A dose of laughter a day, keeps the ugly away."
Wooism

"To laugh often and love much, to appreciate beauty, to find the best in others, to give to oneself... this is to have succeeded."
Ralph Waldo Emerson

"Laughing is my daily victory."
Wooism

"The human race has only one really effective weapon, and that is laughter."
Mark Twain

"We each have this gift... if we assert ourselves with laughter, the sky's the limit."
Wooism

Chapter 3 (Part 2)—LAUGHTER: Laugh a little, laugh a lot. Just don't forget to laugh.

"A laugh is a smile that bursts."
Mary H. Waldrip

"A smile is lovely; as laughter is simply irresistible."
Wooism

"Total absence of humor renders life impossible."
Colette

"I imagine life to be quite dull without laughter. No need to challenge me because I will win."
Wooism

"When you have a heartfelt belly laugh, all parts of your being - the physiological, the psychological, the spiritual – they all vibrate in one single tune. They all vibrate in harmony!"
Osho

"A great laugh is a gift to the mind and to the soul. Side effects: sharp mind, good health, joy and love. There is no reason not to laugh."
Wooism

*"I am thankful for laughter,
except when milk comes out of my nose."*
Woody Allen

*"I am confident to say that laughter keeps me quite young.
Age is just a number."*
Wooism

*"I like the laughter that opens the lips and the heart,
shows at the same time, the pearls and the soul."*
Victor Hugo

"Laughter is charisma, and charisma makes you beautiful."
Wooism

*"If we can learn to laugh unconditionally, our happiness too,
will become unconditional."*
Dr. Madan Kataria

*"Laughter yoga is the best exercise. It's is easy and fun to
do... and it comes with health benefits up the wazoo."*
Wooism

Chapter 3 (Part 2)—LAUGHTER: Laugh a little, laugh a lot. Just don't forget to laugh.

"I'm happy that I have brought laughter because
I have been shown by many the values of it in so many lives,
in so many ways."

Lucille Ball

"The one gift I constantly regift to myself
and to all my friends is laughter."

Wooism

"Laughter is the language of the soul."

Pablo Neruda

"Let's all get along. We can all communicate
with one universal language: Laughter."

Wooism

"There is nothing in the world so irresistibly contagious as
laughter and good humor."

Charles Dickens

"Make me laugh, and I am putty in your hands."

Wooism

"Intention is the active desire and commitment to be happy. It's the decision to consciously choose attitudes and behaviors that lead to happiness over unhappiness."
Rick Foster & Greg Hicks

"My decision is easy. I choose laughter, and my solution is happiness."
Wooism

"I don't trust anyone who doesn't laugh."
Maya Angelou

"I am attracted to happy people."
Wooism

"Comedy is acting out optimism."
Robin Williams

"I love to be around people who laugh often, and I take pride in making others laugh, too."
Wooism

Chapter 3 (Part 2)—LAUGHTER: Laugh a little, laugh a lot. Just don't forget to laugh.

*"Laughter is timeless. Imagination has no age.
And dreams are forever."*
Walt Disney

"With a cheery, happy attitude, laughter
welcomes all the possibilities."
Wooism

*"I love people who make me laugh. I honestly think it's the thing
I like most, to laugh. It cures a multitude of ills. It's probably the
most important thing in a person."*
Audrey Hepburn

"That's all it takes... a little bit of laughter.
A funny person is a sexy person."
Wooism

"A day without laughter is a day wasted."
Charlie Chaplin

"I feel almost selfish to say that I laugh every day."
Wooism

"A man isn't poor if he can still laugh."
Raymond Hitchcock

"Money does not define me. Happiness does."
Wooism

"And we should consider every day lost on which we have not danced at least once. And we should call every truth false which was not accompanied by at least one laugh."
Friedrich Nietzsche

"Experience the power of laughter... To me, laughing is dancing in place and my every being is filled with joy."
Wooism

Chapter 3 (Part 2)—LAUGHTER: Laugh a little, laugh a lot. Just don't forget to laugh.

"*A sense of humor… is needed armor. Joy in one's heart and some laughter on one's lips is a sign that the person down deep has a pretty good grasp of life.*"
Hugh Sidey

"Living life without laughter is living without experiencing happiness."
Wooism

"*If I had no sense of humor I would long ago have committed suicide.*"
Gandhi

"Heavy doses of laughter have kept me sane."
Wooism

*"With the fearful strain that is on me night and day,
if I did not laugh, I should die."*

Abraham Lincoln

*"Stress was never my friend.
Laughter stepped in and saved me."*

Wooism

"To me, there is no picture so beautiful as smiling, bright-eyed children; no music so sweet as their clear and ringing laughter."

P.T. Barnum

"Laughter brings me euphoria, and it's my daily sunshine."

Wooism

"Laughter is the fireworks of the soul."

Josh Billings

"I think it is INSANE not to laugh."

Wooism

CHAPTER FOUR

FREEDOM:
Get rid of your baggage, and let go of negative emotions. Say good bye to the past.

For some, this is one of the biggest challenges they will experience. The past is riddled with emotion that can take anyone on a roller coaster ride. The choice of how you take the ride is yours. Personally, I'd like to take the ride with my hands in the air, laughing all the way. I love my freedom.

freedom:

n. the state of being free or at liberty rather than in confinement or under physical restraint, exemption from external control, the power to determine action without restraint, exemption; immunity: freedom of fear, a liberty taken.

"Happiness depends upon ourselves."
Aristotle

"I used to have an excuse for all my mistakes; I blamed others, or I blamed the past; and I never took ownership for my wrong-doings. Instead I played the victim. Poor me. I repeated the same bad choices again and again, until I realized that I was going nowhere. Once I put forth my intentions to better my life, I was finally able to let go of the past little by little; and today, I move forward with a positive attitude. I am the victor now because my choice is happiness."
Wooism

"We delight in the beauty of the butterfly, but rarely admit the changes it has gone through to achieve that beauty."
Maya Angelou

"Transformation is part of life's journey. When I embrace change, something beautiful happens. I allow myself to learn and grow, and slowly but surely, I become someone better than I was yesterday."
Wooism

er 4—FREEDOM: Get rid of your baggage, and let go of negative emotions. Say good bye to the past.

"Nobody trips over mountains. It is the small pebble that causes you to stumble. Pass all the pebbles in your path, and you will find you have crossed the mountain."

Author Unknown

"I fell, I failed, I cried, I yelled. I realize now that each trying moment was a lesson for me. Here I am today, composed, and moving forward, and I am alive and well."

Wooism

"Without forgiveness, life is governed by an endless cycle of resentment and retaliation."

Roberto Assagiolo

"When I held onto resentment, I was easily angered and I was quite unhappy. I was not capable of laughing on a whim, and I was offended often."

Wooism

"Anger makes you smaller while forgiveness forces you to grow beyond what you are."
Cherie Carter Scott

"Ten years ago, you'd hear the lengthiest stories from me of how I was hurt by so many people from my childhood up to the present. I had every reason to be angry and rebellious. Today, I will tell you the same beginning, but with a different ending. Yes, I have been hurt. We all get hurt. We all experience struggles. I cannot change the past; I cannot change others; however, I can change myself. Forgiveness has allowed me to give my life a different perspective – a good one. At present, I choose to let nothing from my past interfere with the life I make for myself today. I want to be happy, and so I am. I love to be around kind, loving people, and so these are my dear friends today. Simply put, life can be as good as you want it to be."

Wooism

"If we really want to love, we must learn how to forgive."
Mother Teresa

"My heart is filled with so much love that I cannot believe I once hated."
Wooism

*"Mistakes are always forgivable,
if one has the courage to admit them."*
Bruce Lee

"I stay away from denial as denial is the lie that tempts us to stray from our integrity. Denial is just an excuse we use when we do not want to admit something we did wrong. When we take responsibility for our actions, we learn and we grow."
Wooism

"I can change. I can live out my imagination instead of my memory. I can tie myself to a limitless potential instead of my limiting past."
Stephen Covey

"Today's affirmation: I am ready to kick the baggage to the curb. I want my hands free; I want relief."
Wooism

"The more anger towards the past you carry in your heart, the less capable you are of loving in the present."
Barbara de Angelis

"My past was filled with much pain, anger and resentment. Because I finally learned how to let go of the unhealthy emotions, I no longer suffer from self-inflicted emotional abuse; only a memory of the pain remains. My present is filled with so much love and joy; I am thankful that
I am truly at peace."
Wooism

"When you forgive, you in no way change the past – but you sure do change the future."
Bernard Meltzer

"It did not happen overnight... however, when I realized that I had let go of all my grudges, I also realized that it was easy to be happy."
Wooism

"There is only one thing that makes a dream impossible to achieve; the fear of failure."
Paulo Coelho

"The sooner we let go of fear, the sooner we can succeed. Failure is meant to be a lesson, not a deterrent.
Let go, and explore."
Wooism

r 4—FREEDOM: Get rid of your baggage, and let go of negative emotions. Say good bye to the past.

> *"To forgive is to set a prisoner free and discover that the prisoner was you."*
> ### Lewis B. Smedes

"I stand for freedom. By forgiving and letting go of all my negative emotions, I free myself of the heaviness in my heart. I'm given a new-found strength to move on, to love and to explore the beauty that lies before me."
Wooism

"Darkness cannot drive out darkness, only light can do that. Hate cannot drive out hate, only love can do that."
Martin Luther King, Jr.

"Love heals and transforms your pain; it brings goodness and invites more love; ultimately, love is the eternal salvation."
Wooism

"To establish true self-esteem, we must concentrate on our success and forget about the failures and the negatives in our lives."
Denis Waitley

"I have experienced failure; I have made my share of mistakes; and I have wronged and repented. I decide from today forward, to throw away any negative thought, and I shall replace it with a positive one."
Wooism

*"You can't have a better tomorrow if you are
thinking about yesterday all the time."*
Charles F. Kettering

*"From afar, it looks difficult, but once you get started,
life gets easier. Self-improvement is achieved step by step,
so leave behind the disappointments from yesterday,
and plan to succeed today."*
Wooism

*"For every minute you remain angry,
you give up sixty seconds of peace of mind."*
Ralph Waldo Emerson

*"My solution was anger; therefore my result was anger.
For years, I made no progression. When I forgave and freed
myself, my ties with family and friends progressed into
loving, respectful relationships. My end result: love."*
Wooism

er 4—FREEDOM: Get rid of your baggage, and let go of negative emotions. Say good bye to the past.

"Think continually in terms of the rewards of success rather than the penalties of failure."

Brian Tracy

"As I live my life with integrity, I admit my faults, and I admit defeat. Success is my goal, and I'm keeping my eyes on the prize!"

Wooism

"Whatever with the past has gone, the best is always yet to come."

Lucy Larcom

"Life was not always easy. I faced disappointment after disappointment. I came to realize that the choice was mine: continue to sob and complain, or collect myself and move forward. Leaving the past behind was not easy, but the power of positive thinking was my beginning to finding happiness."

Wooism

"It's the greatest gift you can give to yourself, to forgive. Forgive everybody."

Maya Angelou

"One of the most difficult things in my life was the most therapeutic. Forgiveness freed me."

Wooism

"That's old. I'm new. Goodbye."
Glenn Morshower

"What a relief it is to say goodbye to yesterday's misery. Ahh, this is freedom."
Wooism

"Remove all blame from your vocabulary. Catch yourself when you find yourself using your past history as a reason for your failure to act today, and instead say, 'I am free now to detach myself from what I used to be.'"
Dr. Wayne Dyer

"My past does not dictate my future; however, my lessons from the past will."
Wooism

"Man is free at the moment he wishes to be."
François-Marie Arouet
Voltaire

"Every goal and dream of mine can be accomplished through my persistence, my resilience and my conviction. I have the power within myself to make anything happen."
Wooism

*"The weak can never forgive.
Forgiveness is the attribute of the strong."*
Gandhi

"Once you forgive, you will feel relief and you will experience true freedom. Freedom gives you inner strength and puts your heart at ease."
Wooism

"Peace I leave with you; my peace I give you. I do not give you as the world gives. Do not let your hearts be troubled and do not be afraid."
John 14:27

"When you mend your broken heart, you become free and strong; only then, will you be able to give and receive love more passionately."
Wooism

"Finish every day and be done with it. You have done what you could. Some blunders and absurdities no doubt have crept in; forget them as soon as you can. Tomorrow is a new day; begin it well and serenely and with too high a spirit to be cumbered with your old nonsense. This day is all that is good and fair. It is too dear, with its hopes and invitations, to waste a moment on yesterdays."

Ralph Waldo Emerson

"Today is a new day. One positive thought today can free me from the pain and sorrow from yesterday. My affirmation today: Smile... because it's going to be a great day."

Wooism

"Man should forget his anger before he lies down to sleep."

Gandhi

"If I should find myself upset at the end of the night, I meditate or pray. I ask for love and peace. And my results: love and peace."

Wooism

"Anger dwells only in the bosom of fools."

Albert Einstein

"There is not much effort required to be wise. Simply choose happiness."

Wooism

"Never let your memories be greater than your dreams."
Doug Ivester

"I may never forget the past, but nor will I allow my memories to stop me from achieving greatness."
Wooism

"The only limits of our realization of tomorrow will be our doubts of today."
Franklin Delano Roosevelt

"Failure, fear, and hesitation; let them go, and spread your wings and fly far, far away from them. Only then will you achieve success."
Wooism

"Live out your imagination, not your history."
Stephen Covey

"Keep the past in the past; let your thoughts and dreams guide you into the future."
Wooism

"If you are distressed by anything external, the pain is not due to the thing itself, but to your own estimate of it; and this you have the power to revoke at any moment."
Marcus Arelius

"Today's affirmation: I will keep my thoughts, my words and my actions positive. I expect positive results today."
Wooism

"You gain strength, courage, and confidence by every experience in which you stop to look fear in the face. You must do the thing in which you think you cannot do."
Eleanor Roosevelt

"Every trial and every error has prepared me to be stronger and better. I can conquer this task at hand, and I will. I believe in myself, that I am stronger and more confident than ever. No one can take this power away from me."
Wooism

er 4—FREEDOM: Get rid of your baggage, and let go of negative emotions. Say good bye to the past.

"When you haven't forgiven those who've hurt you, you turn back against your future. When you do forgive, you start walking forward."
Tyler Perry

"I have made plenty of mistakes. I have hurt and been hurt. I have forgiven, and I have learned and grown. I choose freedom because I choose happiness."
Wooism

"Failure is the only opportunity to begin again, only this time more wisely."
Henry Ford

"I believe that learning and exploring the possibilities in me are nominal... I believe in self-aid because I believe in a better me."
Wooism

Self-Aid: Inspirations to Turn Struggles into Success

CHAPTER FIVE

ATTITUDE:
Mindset is reflected in your attitude. Make yours one of positive thinking and gratitude.

A good attitude makes up a good personality. I believe that when I have a positive thought, I manifest a positive result, too. I'd much rather have positive things coming my way than negative; therefore, I choose to look at the bright side of things and be grateful. This is my attitude... Mindset is a choice; a good one shows in your zest for life.

attitude:

n. the way you think and feel about someone or something, a feeling or way of thinking that affects a person's behavior

"Two things define you. Your patience when you have nothing, and your attitude when you have everything."
Unknown

"A positive attitude is the difference between a good and a bad day."
Wooism

"Optimism is the faith that leads to achievement. Nothing can be done without hope and confidence."
Helen Keller

"The world is my oyster… There are yet so many things to do, places to see, goals to achieve, and people to meet…. My life is just beginning. I wake up, and I know that the best is yet to come."
Wooism

"I am an optimist. It does not seem too much being anything else."
Winston Churchill

"One positive thought today can show me the vision of all the possibilities of tomorrow."
Wooism

Chapter 5—ATTITUDE: Mindset is reflected in your attitude. Make yours one of positive thinking and gratitude.

"*It's always too soon to quit.*"
Norman Vincent Peale

"Like the Little Engine That Could, 'I can do it.
I can do it. I can do it.' Yes, I can."
Wooism

"*Men succeed when they realize that their failures are the preparation for their victories.*"
Ralph Waldo Emerson

"Failure will not stop me. I am stronger, I am better and I am smarter today than I was yesterday. I am here to win."
Wooism

"*It's a funny thing about life; if you refuse to accept anything but the best, you very often get it.*"
W. Somerset Maugham

"Today's affirmation: I am not mediocre; I am great.
I am not common; I am original. I am not ordinary;
I am extraordinary."
Wooism

"Nothing is impossible; the word itself says 'I'm possible'."
Audrey Hepburn

"I am present; therefore, anything is possible."
Wooism

"Whenever you make a mistake or get knocked down by life, don't look back at it too long. Mistakes are life's way of teaching you. Your capacity for occasional blunders is inseparable from your capacity to reach your goals. No one wins them all, and failures, when they happen, are just part of your growth. Shake off your blunders. How will you know your limits without an occasional failure? Never quit. Your turn will come."
Og Mandino

"With experience, came wisdom. With wisdom, came clarity. With clarity, comes victory."
Wooism

"Our life is what our thoughts make it."
Marcus Arelius

"The power of my mind is stronger than I gave it credit for; my thoughts create my words and my words create my actions. My actions tell the story of my grand and beautiful life."
Wooism

"Try to be a rainbow in someone's cloud."
Maya Angelou

"No effort required… One smile can brighten anyone's day, including your own."
Wooism

"Keep your thoughts positive because your thoughts become your words.

Keep your words positive because your words become your behavior.

Keep your behavior positive because your behavior becomes your habits.

Keep your habits positive because your habits become your values.

Keep you values positive because your values become your destiny."
Gandhi

"Today's affirmation: I have the power of positive thinking. I will smile and think happy thoughts; I will choose my words wisely and follow with my actions. I am living proof that good things happen because of my positive attitude."
Wooism

"Man is made that when anything fires his soul, impossibilities vanish."

Jean De La Fontaine

"The moment you discover your life purpose, you will feel the passion stir inside you; it will bubble up so powerfully, that nothing can stop you from tasting success."

Wooism

"Weakness of attitude becomes weakness of character."

Albert Einstein

"My definition of ugly is a bad attitude."

Wooism

"Nobody can go back and start a new beginning, but anyone can start today and make a new ending."

Maria Robinson

"This is my life. I am the writer and the editor for my life story."

Wooism

"I would rather fail trying than succeed at doing nothing."
Denis Waitley

"I have two options: I can pursue my passion expecting to face challenges along the way, or I can give up now and accept defeat."
Wooism

"There are two primary choices in life: to accept conditions as they exist, or accept the responsibility for changing them."
Denis Waitley

"I am determined to make a difference today. And so be it."
Wooism

"Anyone who has never made a mistake has never tried anything new."
Albert Einstein

"Roadblocks, deterrents, detours: Nothing will stop me. I simply will invent another route."
Wooism

Self-Aid: Inspirations to Turn Struggles into Success

"When you have exhausted all possibilities,
remember this – you haven't."
Thomas Edison

"Today's mindset: Bring it on. Persistence and resilience
defeat any challenge."
Wooism

"If you don't like something, change it. If you can't change it,
change your attitude."
Maya Angelou

"The first option is to sit around and complain today.
Please take the other option."
Wooism

"An intelligent person will open your mind,
a beautiful person will open your eyes and a loving,
kind person will open your heart."
Unknown

"I choose to be around happy people because their energy is
contagious, and I want some of what they have!"
Wooism

Chapter 5—ATTITUDE: Mindset is reflected in your attitude. Make yours one of positive thinking and gratitude.

"Success consists of going from failure to failure without a loss of enthusiasm."
Winston Churchill

"Today's mindset: One fall will not stop me... It's time to get back up and start again. I will persevere... I can see the winner's circle straight ahead."
Wooism

"Excellence is not an exception; it is a prevailing attitude."
Colin Powell

"Once I set my mind to 'positive', the results become predictable."
Wooism

"Never, never, never give up."
Winston Churchill

"Failure has awakened the beast in me; I now want to take charge, and go after what belongs to me, for my prize awaits me."
Wooism

"We can change our future by merely changing our attitude to the positive. Simple yet powerful."
Zeenat Merchant Syal

"Once you tap into a habit of positive thinking, you will realize that you have the power to heal, change, and make this world a better place to live."
Wooism

"Your smile will give you a positive countenance that will make people feel comfortable around you."
Les Brown

"One happy face deserves another. Give one smile and pay it forward, as it causes a happy domino effect."
Wooism

"To succeed, you need to find something to hold on to, something to motivate you, something to inspire you."
Tony Dorsett

"One inspiration a day lifts my spirit. It changes my mood instantly, and it gives me the power to manifest the outcome that I want."
Wooism

"It takes but one positive thought when given a chance to survive and thrive to overpower an entire army of negative thoughts."

Robert H. Schuller

"When the good angel and bad angel jump onto our shoulders, we often choose the enticing one; he's convincing yet unscrupulous... Those who are fed up with repeating the same mistakes learn to make a habit of replacing their bad thoughts with good ones — this is when progress begins."

Wooism

"In order to carry a positive action we must develop here a positive vision."

Dalai Lama

"The power of our thought is stronger than we can imagine. With our thoughts, we can create a reality."

Wooism

"We are what we think. All that we are arises with our thoughts. With our thoughts, we make the world."

Buddha

"When we habitually think positive thoughts and follow them with positive words and actions, we are on our way to making a positive difference."

Wooism

*"Yesterday is not ours to recover,
but tomorrow is ours to win or lose."*
Lyndon B. Johnson

"Today's affirmation: I shall not dwell on the past.
It is up to me to create my destiny."
Wooism

Always Do Your Best. Your best is going to change from moment to moment; it will be different when you are healthy as opposed to sick. Under any circumstance, simply do your best, and you will avoid self-judgment, self-abuse and regret."
Miguel Angel Ruiz

"Today's affirmation: I am special. I am enough."
Wooism

"We are shaped by our thoughts; we become what we think. When the mind is pure, joy follows like a shadow that never leaves."
Buddha

"It never fails; a positive attitude brings me positive results."
Wooism

"Your attitude is like a box of crayons that color your world. Constantly color your picture gray, and your picture will always be bleak. Try adding some bright colors to the picture by including humor, and your picture begins to lighten up."
Allen Klein

"A positive thought, a smile, a laugh, a sweet gesture, a kind deed: these are some of the things we can do daily to make our day a little more colorful and a lot brighter."
Wooism

"Keep your face to the sunshine and you cannot see a shadow."
Helen Keller

"Positive thinking takes some practice;
but once you start, you keep progressing.
Tomorrow's forecast is sunny and warm."
Wooism

"Find a place inside where there's joy,
and the joy will burn out the pain."
Joseph Campbell

"Sometimes I need a reminder of the little things that make me smile. I close my eyes, think of something sweet, and multiply that by ten. I open my eyes, laugh a little and feel inspired that things will get better."
Wooism

"Insanity: Doing the same thing over and over again and expecting different results."
Albert Einstein

"Good things come from making mistakes. I've learned, I've grown, and I've changed. Lo and behold: Magic."
Wooism

CHAPTER SIX

INTEGRITY:
I am what I say I am, and I let my actions define me.

I am honest, I speak my truth, I follow through on my promises, and I live my life as I would hope others might do the same from my example. I live a life of integrity, and I am proud of it.

integrity:

n. noun . The quality of being honest and having strong moral principles, moral uprightness.

Synonyms: honesty, probity, rectitude, honor, good character, principle(s), ethics, morals, righteousness, morality, virtue, decency, fairness, scrupulousness, sincerity, truthfulness, trustworthiness,

"Always aim at complete harmony of thought and word and deed. Always aim at purifying your thoughts and everything will be well."

Gandhi

"View integrity to be your most prized possession. Being a good person starts with your thoughts and ends with your actions."

Wooism

"I stand for honesty, equality, kindness, compassion, treating people the way you want to be treated, and helping those in need. To me, those are the traditional values."

Ellen DeGeneres

"The Golden Rule is the universal language: "Do unto others as you wish them to do unto you. Being a genuinely kind and loving person makes you beautiful."

Wooism

Chapter 6—INTEGRITY: I am what I say I am, and I let my actions define me.

"Be Impeccable With Your Word. Speak with integrity. Say only what you mean. Avoid using the word to speak against yourself or to gossip about others. Use the power of your word in the direction of truth and love."
Miguel Angel Ruiz

"I live by fairness for all, even if it makes my battle more difficult. I defend those who are mistreated, and I will fight with fairness even if those around me stay quiet. I choose to be transparent and stay true to myself. Situations change, but I do not. Most of all, I never say one thing and do another. This is my word; and there will be no compromise."
Wooism

"I have always tried to be true to myself, to pick those battles I thought were important. My ultimate responsibility is to myself. I could never be anything else."
Arthur Ashe

"I am authentic. What you see is what you get. I do as I say, and I say as I do. If you choose to judge me, I ask that you do not judge me for my appearance but rather for what I stand for, through my words and my actions."
Wooism

"Whatever words we utter should be chosen with care for people will hear them and be influenced by them for good or ill."
Buddha

"My words are chosen wisely, as once they are spoken, they are heard. My words are powerful because they stand for truth."
Wooism

"The greatness of a man is not in how much wealth he acquires, but in his integrity and his ability to affect those around him positively."
Bob Marley

"These are the qualities of a good character: one who acts with integrity, exudes kindness, generosity and moral courage; one who treats others well and has strong conviction. A person with good character will always have a positive effect on others."
Wooism

Chapter 6—INTEGRITY: I am what I say I am, and I let my actions define me.

"Achievement of your happiness is the only moral purpose of your life, and that happiness, not pain or mindless self-indulgence, is the proof of your moral integrity, since it is the proof and the result of your loyalty to the achievement of your values."

Ayn Rand

"I value my words and my actions. When I speak and when I act, my concern is not what others think of me. Rather, my concern is what I think of myself. I live authentically, and I live with true passion to do what is right and good for all."

Wooism

"Live so that when your children think of fairness, caring, and integrity, they think of you."

H. Jackson Brown, Jr.

"I care deeply that my child has the same respect for me as I do for myself."

Wooism

"With integrity, you have nothing to fear, since you have nothing to hide. With integrity, you will do the right thing, so you will have no guilt."

Zig Ziglar

"Integrity consists of the fundamental values that I believe in and choose to live by daily. I have made mistakes, and I have corrected my wrongs. I take full responsibility for my actions and feel no guilt today because I have nothing to hide. I am grateful to be consistent in my words and actions alike."

Wooism

"We learned about honesty and integrity – that the truth matters... that you don't take shortcuts or play by your own set of rules... and success doesn't count unless you earn it fair and square."

Michelle Obama

"True success is accomplished when you stay honest and act on moral principles."

Wooism

Chapter 6—INTEGRITY: I am what I say I am, and I let my actions define me.

"Let me define a leader. He must have vision and passion and not be afraid of any problem. Instead, he should know how to defeat it. Most importantly, he must work with integrity."
P. J. Abdul Kalam

"With passion and integrity, you will find harmony in body, mind and soul; this is when greatness is achieved."
Wooism

"The strength of a nation derives from the integrity of the home."
Confucius

"One's moral fiber is the structure of his character. It is the DNA of one's personality."
Wooism

"Real integrity is doing the right thing, knowing that nobody's going to know whether you did it or not."
Oprah Winfrey

"By being true to yourself, you will find that everywhere you go, you are just that: your authentic self. You need not adjust your character for anyone."
Wooism

"Honesty and integrity are absolutely essential for success in life – all areas of life. The really good news is that anyone can develop both honesty and integrity.

Zig Ziglar

"It does not take much effort to be a good person. All we need to have is a little desire."

Wooism

"Have the courage to say no. Have the courage to face the truth. Do the right thing because it is right. These are the magic keys to living your life with integrity."

W. Clement Stone

"Your self-respect can never be damaged because integrity speaks volumes."

Wooism

"The greatness of a man is not in how much wealth he acquires, but in his integrity and his ability to affect those around him positively."

Bob Marley

"Honesty and integrity are not malleable; they follow your character in sickness or in health, for richer or poorer."

Wooism

Chapter 6—INTEGRITY: I am what I say I am, and I let my actions define me.

"*All that we are is the result of what we have thought. If a man speaks or acts with an evil thought, pain follows him. If a man speaks or acts with a pure thought, happiness follows him, like a shadow that never leaves him.*"
Buddha

"Living a life with integrity is part of my moral fiber. My convictions are storng; they cannot be compromised. My character is honor and complete honesty manifested through my thoughts, words and deeds."
Wooism

"*We make a living by what we get.
We make a life by what we give.*"
Winston Churchill

"There are no expectations when giving from your heart."
Wooism

"*The supreme quality for leadership is unquestionably integrity. Without it, no real success is possible, no matter whether it is on a section gang, a football field, in an army, or in an office.*"
Dwight D. Eisenhower

"People who succeed greatly without compromising their integrity are the most inspirational leaders of the world."
Wooism

"My country is my world, and my religion is to do good."
Ralph Waldo Emerson

"One word to describe my religion: Integrity."
Wooism

"Keep your thoughts positive because your thoughts become your words. Keep your words positive because your words become your behaviors. Keep your behaviors positive because your behaviors become your habits. Keep your habits positive because your habits become your values. Keep your values positive because your values become your destiny."
Gandhi

"Positive thoughts, in combination with positive action, always lead to a positive outcome. There is always room for improvement. Practicing to be a better person physically, mentally and spiritually is a work in progress."
Wooism

Chapter 6—INTEGRITY: I am what I say I am, and I let my actions define me.

"Action expresses priorities."
Gandhi

"Words are useless if they are not justified with actions."
Wooism

"Kind words can be short and easy to speak,
but their echoes are truly endless."
Mother Teresa

"The power of the word can change the world."
Wooism

'Thought is the blossom; language the bud;
action the fruit behind it."
Ralph Waldo Emerson

"The answers come in leaps and bounds when your thoughts, words and actions are in sync; this is when you know that you are living your life purpose."
Wooism

Self-Aid: Inspirations to Turn Struggles into Success

CHAPTER SEVEN

DREAM:
My life is the result of my dreams.

I live according to what I feel my purpose is. I dream big and I live big. My passion is living my dream.

dream:

n. an aspiration; a goal; an aim

v. to have a dream, to imagine as possible; to conceive, to bring imagination into reality.

"I choose to make the rest of my life the best of my life."
Louise Hay

"This is my life. No one can live it for me. Only I can make this life the best life imaginable; and I will."
Wooism

"If you can dream it, you can achieve it."
Zig Ziglar

"I believe that every thought and every idea can be put into action and lived out through my reality."
Wooism

"Life is either a daring adventure or nothing."
Helen Keller

"When you find your life purpose, you realize that everything you do and strive for is no longer work but true enjoyment."
Wooism

Chapter 7—DREAM: My life is the result of my dreams.

*"The future belongs to those who believe
in the beauty of their dreams."*
Eleanor Roosevelt

"My aspirations and dreams include all the little things that create the bigger goal that I wish to attain. Living each day to my fullest potential brings out the wonders and the magic of my days. I am happy to be living my dream."
Wooism

"Happiness is not something you postpone for the future; it is something you design for the present."
Jim Rohn

"Once you discover your purpose here on earth, you start enjoying all the little moments of your journey."
Wooism

"Think of yourself as on a threshold of unparalleled success. A whole, clear, glorious life lies before you. Achieve! Achieve!"
Andrew Carnegie

"Success starts when you leave the excuses behind and acknowledge that you can change. It is then that you begin your journey to greatness and experience victory."
Wooism

*"Passion is energy. Feel the power that comes
from focusing on what excites you."*
Oprah Winfrey

*"Love creates passion. If you have passion for a better
tomorrow, anything is possible."*
Wooism

*"To be successful, you don't need a beautiful face or a heroic
body. What you need is a skillful mind and the ability to perform."*
Mr. Bean

*"Everything that we want to achieve and every dream
of ours can become a reality, if we learn to put
our thoughts into action."*
Wooism

*"To make your dreams come true, you must go to the unseen
world – the world of spirit or inspiration. It is in this world that
will guide you to anything you'd like to have in your life."*
Dr. Wayne Dyer

*"The mind is a powerful tool. You are capable of creating
greatness through imagination. When you master your
thoughts, you manifest your reality."*
Wooism

Chapter 7—DREAM: My life is the result of my dreams.

"Work like you don't need the money. Love like you've never been hurt. Dance like nobody is watching."
Mark Twain

"Put a little passion into every thought and action; you will ultimately create the amazement that is the outcome of your dreams."
Wooism

"And in the end, it's not the years in your life that count. It's the life in your years."
Abraham Lincoln

"When I die, I hope to leave behind a legacy. Most importantly, I hope to be remembered for living my life to the fullest; living purposefully and passionately through my thoughts and my words. I hope to be remembered as a woman of conviction."
Wooism

"To laugh often and much; to win the respect of intelligent people and the affection of children; to earn the appreciation of honest critics and to endure the betrayal of false friends; to appreciate beauty; to find the best in others; to leave the world a bit better whether by a healthy child, a garden patch or a redeemed social condition; to know even one life has breathed easier because you have lived. This is to have succeeded."

Ralph Waldo Emerson

"To have been true to yourself throughout your failures and your victories and to have made a positive difference in one's life is to have lived a good life."

Wooism

'Thought is the blossom; language the bud; action the fruit behind it."

Ralph Waldo Emerson

"Answers come in leaps and bounds when your thoughts, words and actions are in sync; this is when you know that you are living your life purpose."

Wooism

Chapter 7—DREAM: My life is the result of my dreams.

"Where there is love, there is life."
Gandhi

"Love is powerful. For those who disagree that love conquers all, you have not discovered the power that love brings to your every desire. Find the power from within, and you will live your dream."
Wooism

"I am easily satisfied with the very best."
Winston Churchill

"The combination of effort and passion brings endless possibilities."
Wooism

"Life is one grand, sweet song, so start the music."
Ronald Reagan

"When opportunity arrives, make sure you let it pick you up and fly you to the stars."
Wooism

*"Imagination is everything.
It is the preview of life's coming events."*

Albert Einstein

"It is a wondrous yet inexplicable discovery that thoughts manifest your destiny."

Wooism

"Be the change that you want to see in this world."

Gandhi

"Be the light that you wish to have shone upon you. Inspire as you wish to be inspired. You are the difference this world needs today."

Wooism

"My life is my message"

Gandhi

"Throughout your life journey, may you come to a realization that there is no difference between living your life and your dream. Each is one of the same."

Wooism

Chapter 7—DREAM: My life is the result of my dreams.

"Be kind to one another."
Ellen DeGeneres

"Success is not calculated by the amount of money you have in your bank account. True success exists when you find harmony in your soul; when you do not hesitate to defend injustice; and when you choose to do unto others as you wish them to do unto you."
Wooism

"I know in my heart that man is good, that what is right will always eventually triumph. And there's purpose and worth to each and every life."
Ronald Reagan

"We are given life to shine and make a difference. If we can learn to explore the light within ourselves, we can light up the world."
Wooism

"There are no secrets to success. It is the result of preparation, hard work, and learning from failure."
Colin Powell

"Failure has fueled my passion. I will win my next battles, and I will settle for nothing less."
Wooism

"Whatever you are, be a good one."
Abraham Lincoln

"This is my dream; to be the best me that I can be."
Wooism

"I am thankful for all those who said NO to me. It's because of them I'm doing it myself."
Albert Einstein

"For the supportive family and friends who stood by me, and for those who lost faith in me and walked away when things were difficult: I thank you for giving me the strength to believe in myself, to learn to be capable, to learn to succeed independently; and ultimately, I thank you for giving me the freedom to find my dream. Thank you for reminding me that I am strong, and I am whole."
Wooism

Chapter 7—DREAM: My life is the result of my dreams.

*"The only thing that will stop you
from fulfilling your dreams is you."*
Tom Bradley

*"My worth is my success, as it determines my wealth.
The true measure of my wealth is not how much money
I have, but how worthy I am after losing it all."*
Wooism

*"We always attract into our lives whatever we think about
most, believe in strongly, expect on the deepest level, and
imagine most vividly."*
Shakti Gawain

*"Imagination is a powerful gift. The power of my thoughts
with my actions can change every situation from dim to
bright in an instance."*
Wooism

*"Success is not the key to happiness. Happiness is the key to
success. If you love what you are doing, you will be successful."*
Albert Schweitzer

*"The key to life is to search for happiness; and success will
soon follow. Only then will dreams become reality."*
Wooism

"Dreams are illustrations...
from the book your soul is writing about you."
Marsha Normam

"Today's affirmation: I am made up of energy. I alone can use this energy to manifest my dreams and desires."
Wooism

"All our dreams can come true,
if we have the courage to pursue them."
Walt Disney

"Magic happens when we allow
our imagination to join forces with our passion."
Wooism

"So many of our dreams at first seem impossible, then they seem probable, and then, when we summon the will, they soon become inevitable."
Christopher Reeve

"Miracles happen every day, but only for people who have the imagination to believe in miracles and the insight to look for them."
Wooism

Chapter 7—DREAM: My life is the result of my dreams.

"Every calling is great when greatly pursued."
Oliver Wendall Holmes

*"Each and every one of us has a life purpose.
Once we find it, the journey becomes more exciting,
and the dream comes to life."*
Wooism

"To believe in something and not live it, is dishonest."
Gandhi

*"Embrace the gift that you were given. This is your life,
your gift. Use your gift wisely and the world
will be graced with your presence."*
Wooism

"Don't be afraid to see what you see."
Albert Einstein

"Follow your vision, and live your dream."
Wooism

Self-Aid: Inspirations to Turn Struggles into Success

*"Imagination is the beginning of creation.
You imagine what you desire, you will what you imagine,
and at last, you create what you will."*

George Bernard Shaw

*"There is a message within each and every one of us.
Let's learn to embrace the message; live it,
and share it with the world."*

Wooism

"Never put off till tomorrow what you can do today."

Thomas Jefferson

*"Today's affirmation: I am capable of making my dreams
come true. I have the ability to create greatness."*

Wooism

*"I like the dreams of the future
better than the history of the past."*

Thomas Jefferson

*"Do not look backwards except to correct an error or a
misstep. The light is nearing; it's at the end of this tunnel...
it's time to move forward, full steam ahead."*

Wooism

"'If you can', said Jesus. 'Everything is possible for him who believes.'"

Mark 9:23

"Having faith is a big part of my existence. Faith gives me strength and persistence and determination to achieve my dreams. Faith has shown me that anything is possible."

Wooism

"Happiness is when what you think, what you say, and what you do are in harmony."

Gandhi

"When you live your life to your fullest potential, while staying true to yourself and enjoying the process, you discover that you want to spend the rest of your life doing more of it; this is when you know that you are living your dream."

Wooism

Self-Aid: Inspirations to Turn Struggles into Success

GRATITUDE:
**Every day is Thanksgiving.
Today's affirmation: I will have
an attitude of gratitude.**

gratitude:

*n. thankfulness, gratefulness,
appreciation, the quality of feeling
or being thankful; readiness to show
appreciation for and to return kindness;
feeling or attitude in acknowledging of
a benefit that one has received or will
receive*

"As we express our gratitude, we must never forget that the highest appreciation is not to utter words, but to live by them."

John F. Kennedy

"I have undergone experiences that have tested the limits and the core of my being. Not only have I survived, I have learned and grown significantly. I have a new-found strength and resilience. I have more confidence and persistence. Most of all, I have true faith in myself and in my Higher Power; this faith has made me a believer in miracles. For this, I am very grateful."

Wooism

"Gratitude teaches us to appreciate the rainbow and the storm."

Christina G. Hibbert, Psy. D.

"When I was at my lowest point, I felt the world crashing down on me and it kept tumbling down so hard and so fast... I asked often, 'Why me? How much more can I endure?' Today, I conquer my challenges with a different attitude. I've learned that in order to get positive results, I must change my attitude to a positive one. I am very grateful for my lessons. I was given many tests, and by God, I think I passed!"

Wooism

"We learned about gratitude and humility – that so many people had a hand in our success, from the teachers who inspired us to the janitors who kept our school clean... and we were taught to value everyone's contribution and treat everyone with respect."

Michelle Obama

"I am grateful for everyone who has graced my life. I appreciate every person and everything that crosses my path, as each influence plays a part in my life journey and takes me exactly where I need to be today."

Wooism

"We often take for granted the very things that most deserve our gratitude."

Cynthia Ozick

"In our day-to-day lives, we work, we move fast, we run late for our appointments; we try to finish all the tasks on our lists by the end of the day. Sometimes we forget to say thank you for the smallest gifts. It takes only one second to utter the words 'thank you'. Thank you for another day. Thank you for this delicious cup of espresso. Thank you for your smile. Thank you for the skies. Thank you for the light of the day and the stars in the night. Thank you."

Wooism

"When I admire the wonders of a sunset or the beauty of the moon, my soul expands in the worship of the Creator."
Gandhi

"I draw open the curtains and look out the window.
I look up and see the white clouds against the pretty blue sky.
I hear birds chirping and dogs barking, my espresso brewing
in the kitchen, and my kid playing and hollering in the
background. I inhale deeply... and I exhale.
Oh yes, it feels so good to be alive."
Wooism

"It's not the material things that make us a person;
it's the experiences that we live out."
Richard M. Krawczyk

"After hitting rock bottom, I thought I had lost everything.
No more properties, no more designer clothes;
no more luxuries. My life was empty. I was forced
to take a better look at myself; I was left with the bare
necessities. Then, I found love, faith and hope.
These are the things that came to light once the darkness
lifted. Love, Faith and Hope have made me whole.
Wooism

Chapter 8: GRATITUDE: Every day is Thanksgiving. Today's affirmation: I will have an attitude of gratitude.

"Life is a pure flame, and we live by an invisible sun within us."
Sir Thomas Brown

"Be thankful for when you've been lost in the wilderness. It becomes the compass of life that helps you find your way."
Wooism

"Feeling gratitude and not expressing it is like wrapping a present and not giving it."
William Arthur Ward

"Gratitude is a positive feeling that comes from appreciation; the more you express it, the more comes back to you."
Wooism

"Gratitude is the most exquisite form of courtesy."
Jacques Maritain

"Gratitude displays love and spreads joy."
Wooism

"Never lose an opportunity of seeing anything that is beautiful; for beauty is God's handwriting — a wayside sacrament. Welcome it in every fair face, in every fair sky, in every fair flower, and thank God for it as a cup of blessing."

Ralph Waldo Emerson

"I am grateful for people who are kind and generous and who make me smile by sharing their smile. I am grateful that goodness exists."

Wooism

"I just thank God for all of the blessings."

James Brown

"I am thankful for all the little miracles that have landed on my doorsteps throughout the years. I am thankful that I believe in miracles today. I know that there are more to come."

Wooism

*"It's not happy people who are thankful.
It is thankful people who are happy."*
Author Unknown

"I am thankful for my days, for my nights and all the experiences I've had thus far. I am thankful for learning how to stay strong and persistent throughout my struggles. I am thankful for the little things that have become important in my life. I am thankful for every person who I have encountered throughout my life, for I am who I am today because of you; and I am happy."
Wooism

*"Gratitude is not only the greatest of the virtues,
but the parent of all the others."*
Marcus Tullius Cicero

"A great day can be achieved easily
with an attitude of gratitude."
Wooism

*"To speak gratitude is courteous and pleasant,
to enact gratitude is generous and noble,
but to live gratitude is to touch heaven."*
Johannes A. Gaertner

*"Gratitude comes from the core of my being.
I gratefully share my love and my truth."*
Wooism

*"Gratitude helps you to grow and expand;
gratitude brings joy and laughter into your life and
into the lives of all those around you."*
Eileen Caddy

*"One who expresses gratitude exudes beauty
because she dwells in happiness."*
Wooism

Chapter 8: GRATITUDE: Every day is Thanksgiving. Today's affirmation: I will have an attitude of gratitude.

"Gratitude unlocks the fullness of life. It turns what we have into enough, and more. It turns denial into acceptance, chaos into order, confusion into clarity. It can turn a meal into a feast, a house into a home, a stranger into a friend. Gratitude makes sense of our past, brings peace for today, and creates a vision for tomorrow."

Melody Beattie

"Gratitude heals yesterday's sorrow and brings hope for today and tomorrow."

Wooism

"Oh, give thanks to the Lord, for He is good; His love and His kindness go on forever."

1 Chronicles 16:34

"Thank you for mending me when I was broken; thank you for shedding Light upon me when I was lost. Thank you for giving me faith when I was hopeless. I thank you God, for teaching me the true power of love."

Wooism

"It is through gratitude for the present moment that the spiritual dimension of life opens up."

Eckhart Tolle

"I am grateful that I fell in so deep, because I discovered my wings."

Wooism

"Develop an attitude of gratitude, and give thanks for everything that happens to you, knowing that every step forward is a step toward achieving something bigger and better than your current situation."

Brian Tracy

"From my experiences I found my inner strength. I am grateful that I am wiser today than I was yesterday. I know now that it takes a positive attitude when facing any challenge."

Wooism

"Your children will see what you're all about by what you live rather than by what you say."

Wayne Dyer

"Gratitude, like integrity, is action that comes from the heart. Everyone sees it."

Wooism

*"Gratitude helps you to grow and expand;
gratitude brings joy and laughter into your life and
into the lives of all those around you."*

Eileen Caddy

"Giving thanks is sending good energy out into the world.
An abundance of love and joy comes back to you;
there is no reason to ever stop giving."

Wooism

*"God gave you a gift of 86,400 seconds today.
Have you used one to say 'thank you'?"*

William A. Ward

"Gratitude is a good habit; it is also the sweetest
and most genuine gift to offer."

Wooism

*"For each new morning with its light,
For rest and shelter of the night.
For health and food, for love and friends,
For everything Thy goodness sends."*
Ralph Waldo Emerson

*"For you who came and rescued me when I was lost;
you picked me up when I fell hard. I was silent, but yet you knew. You looked at me and saw my pain. You showed me kindness, and empathy, too. Thank you for caring, thank you for being you. I am blessed to call you 'friend',
as you are true, through and through."*
Wooism

"Enough is a feast."
Buddhist Proverb

"My life is worth a multitude of gratitude."
Wooism

*"For today and its blessings,
I owe the world an attitude of gratitude."*
Clarence E. Hodges

*"Simply put, two words describe how happy
I am to be alive. Thank you."*
Wooism

Chapter 8: GRATITUDE: Every day is Thanksgiving. Today's affirmation: I will have an attitude of gratitude.

"*Lord, make me an instrument of your peace; where there is hatred, let me sow love; where there is injury, pardon; where there is doubt, faith; where there is despair, hope; where there is darkness, light; and where there is sadness, joy.*"

St Francis of Assisi

"Throughout this journey, I have reached my highest highs and I have fallen to my lowest lows. It took a lot of trial and error, but I am grateful for finally discovering the goodness within myself. Thank you, each lesson, for teaching me to endure through hard times. Thank you for teaching me to uphold my integrity with each success. I am privileged to have been enlightened by finding my spirituality. Now I hope to spend the rest of my life expressing my gratitude."

Wooism

"*Gratitude is the music of the heart, when its chords are swept by the breeze of kindness.*"

AuthorUnknown

"Simply uttering the words 'thank you' brings joy to others. I take pleasure in being able to make someone happy."

Wooism

"Gratitude is the fairest blossom which springs from the soul."
Henry Ward Beecher

"When you express gratitude, you express love. When you express love, your light shines from within your soul."
Wooism

"We often take for granted the very things that most deserve our gratitude."
Cynthia Ozick

"Do not ignore the uniqueness that you are, for you alone carry the qualities that make you different from the rest. Always appreciate yourself and be grateful for you are a special gift."
Wooism

"It is through gratitude for the present moment that the spiritual dimension of life opens up."
Eckhart Tolle

"We each have the power in our own ability to turn a wrong into a right, to turn a bad into a good. It is pure gratification to know that I can make a positive difference."
Wooism

POSTSCRIPT

Thank you for reading through the pages of this book and for letting me share my thoughts with you.

I hope that these words have inspired you and that they will continue to encourage you to be the best that you can be.

It's time to explore the possibilities; find your passion and live your dream.

May you find your light and shine with all the brilliance that is you.

Enjoy each moment and don't forget to laugh a little, laugh a lot—laugh your way to Kingdom Come!

Helen

Self-Aid: Inspirations to Turn Struggles into Success

ABOUT THE AUTHOR

Inspirational speaker, author, and radio personality, Helen Woo is passionate about making a positive difference in this world. She openly shares her experiences with the hope that her life lessons will help you to overcome your life challenges.

Helen knows that her life purpose is to inspire and encourage others with her sunny disposition and positive attitude.

As host of a weekly radio talk show called, *"Self Aid Success Stories,"* Woo inspires listeners to laugh a little. Laughter is indeed the best medicine. All challenges can be overcome, starting with *"Self-Aid"*.

The show is jam packed with guests sharing their own inspirational stories of triumph over life's challenges.

Additional information about Helen Woo
Helen Woo has overcome a multitude of incredibly challenging experiences throughout her life. Though it may be easier said than done, she believes that letting go of the baggage and moving on with a positive attitude is vital to achieving success in all areas.

Woo believes that all struggles can be conquered. Every day can and will bring positive change to all who are committed to flourishing and rising above. After all, everyone has a success story! Helen's mission in life is to help others triumph. Using her *Self-Aid* program, Helen Woo supports others in the discovery of their next steps on the path to living their life purpose and achieving their personal and business success.

www.SelfAidwithHelenWoo.com
www.HelenWooToday.com

BOOK REVIEW

Self-Aid—Inspirations to Turn Struggles into Success

Helen Woo's life is devoted to personal triumph over adversarial conditions. Self-Aid means not looking for others to "fix" the problem. Helen takes the idea of blaming others, and removes it from our life playbook. This proactive pathway to healing works beautifully. Thank you, Helen, for reminding us to help ourselves.

— **Glenn Morshower,** Actor, Motivational Speaker, Creator of ***The Extra Mile***

Helen Woo is not just writing from a distant point of observation. She has lived the struggle; felt the pain, experienced moments of defeat, fought the fight, survived and now, has thrived. Her authentic empathetic nature is a reflection of a genuine soul who has found a new beginning in her desire to help others. Helen is refreshingly open and honest about the barriers that she placed in her own path. In this book, *Self-Aid— Inspirations to Turn Struggles into Success*, she shares the tools she used to tear down those blockades, repaving the road that leads to her success. Helen Woo's sincere wish is to share that strategy with others. This book is a gift of the heart.

—**Karen Bailey** Senior Vice President,
Original Programming
Starz Entertainment, LLC,
Starz Media, LLC

Self-Aid—Inspirations to Turn Struggles into Success, by Helen Woo, is filled with strong, powerful words of wisdom, nuggets of life changing courage, and deep empowering insights into life. This book will help propel you into your highest vision for yourself.

—**Kim Somers Egelsee**
#1 Best Selling author,
Getting Your Life to a Ten+

CPSIA information can be obtained at www.ICGtesting.com
Printed in the USA
LVOW12s2048060415

433483LV00001B/20/P